First Facts®

OUR PLACE IN THE UNIVERSE

THE SUN AND STARS

by Ellen Labrecque

CAPSTONE PRESS
a capstone imprint

First Facts is published by Capstone
1710 Roe Crest Drive, North Mankato, Minnesota 56003
www.mycapstone.com

Library of Congress Cataloging-in-Publication Data

Names: Labrecque, Ellen, author.
Title: The sun and stars / by Ellen Labrecque.
Description: North Mankato, Minnesota : an imprint of Pebble, [2020] |
   Series: First facts. Our place in the universe | Audience: Ages 6-9. |
   Audience: K to grade 3.
Identifiers: LCCN 2018056097| ISBN 9781977108470 (hardcover) | ISBN
   9781977110176 (pbk.) | ISBN 9781977108647 (ebook pdf)
Subjects: LCSH: Stars--Juvenile literature. | Sun--Juvenile literature.
Classification: LCC QB801.7 .L3285 2020 | DDC 523.7--dc23
LC record available at https://lccn.loc.gov/2018056097

Editorial Credits
Hank Musolf, editor; Kyle Grenz, designer; Jo Miller, media researcher; Kathy McColley, production
specialist

Photo Credits
ESO/T.Preibisch, 22–23; NASA, Cover; Science Source: Claus Lunau, 9; Shutterstock: Aliona Ursu, 13,
Elena11, 17, isak55, 19 (Top), Kaiskynet Studio, 19 (Bottom), Roxana Bashyrova, 7, Speranto, 7 (Inset),
Volodymyr Goinyk, 11, Sunti, 14, Veronika By, 15 (Insets, all), yanik88, 5, Zakharchuk, 21

Design Elements
Capstone; Shutterstock: Alex Mit, Dimonika, Kanate

All internet sites appearing in back matter were available and accurate when this book was sent to press.

Printed and bound in China.
1671

Table of Contents

Let There Be Light

Stars are like lamps in our sky. They are blazing balls made up of very hot gas. They make their own light. They make our dark sky bright.

Our sun is a star. Eight planets **orbit** around the sun. Earth is one of these eight. Let's learn about the sun and other stars that light up the night sky!

orbit—to travel around an object in space

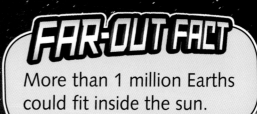

FAR-OUT FACT

More than 1 million Earths could fit inside the sun.

Star Light, Star Bright

We can see thousands of stars when we look into the night sky. There are trillions more in the **universe**.

A star is made up mostly of a gas called **hydrogen**. This gas makes **energy**. The energy turns into light that we can see. It also turns into heat that we can feel.

energy—the ability to do work, such as moving things or giving heat or light

hydrogen—a colorless, odorless, flammable gas

universe—everything that exists, including the Earth, the stars, and all of space

Drawing Stars

Stars are round like planets. Yet we draw stars with five points. Why? A bright star looks like it has lines coming out of it. These lines are rays of light. They aren't really there. Our eyes just see them that way.

A Star Is Born

A star is born in a giant cloud of dust and gas. This cloud is called a **nebula**. The dust and gas mix together. When they mix together, they heat up. This happens over millions of years. Finally, a star is born!

Stars can live for millions, billions, or even trillions of years. The bigger the star, the shorter it lives. The smaller the star, the longer it lives.

nebula—a cloud of dust and gas

A Star Being Born

Dust begins to clump together under the pressure of its own gravity.

gravity—a force that pulls objects together

The material forms a disk as it spirals inward.

The material spirals in to the center, forming the star.

9

The Sun

Our sun is a middle-aged star. It is almost 5 billion years old. **Scientists** think it will live for 5 billion more years.

Our sun is the biggest object in our **solar system**. It is also the hottest. The sun's surface temperature is 11,000 degrees Fahrenheit (6,090 degrees Celsius). It is 80 times more sizzling than the hottest place on Earth.

scientist—an expert in the field of science

solar system—the sun and the eight planets and other bodies that revolve around it

All Sizes and Colors

Stars come in different sizes. The sun seems gigantic. But the sun is a medium-sized star. Stars that are smaller than the sun are called dwarf stars.

FAR-OUT FACT

The stars you can see with just your eyes are much bigger than the sun. They look small because they are so far away.

Stars that are bigger than the sun are called giant stars. Giant stars are 200 times wider than the sun. Supergiant and hypergiant stars are the biggest stars of all. Some are 2,000 times wider than the sun.

Hypergiant star

Supergiant star

Sun

Giant star

Dwarf star

Stars come in different colors. A star's color shows how hot it is. A blue star is the hottest star. It is almost 600 times hotter than Earth. A red star is the least hot. But it is still 50 times hotter than Earth. On a clear night, you can see some of the stars' different colors using a **telescope**.

telescope—a tool that makes faraway things look closer than they are

Temperature of Stars

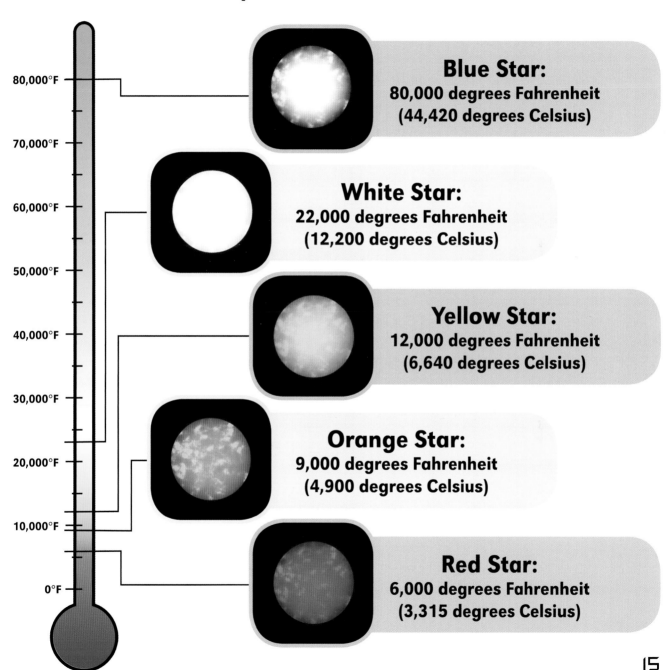

Blue Star:
80,000 degrees Fahrenheit
(44,420 degrees Celsius)

White Star:
22,000 degrees Fahrenheit
(12,200 degrees Celsius)

Yellow Star:
12,000 degrees Fahrenheit
(6,640 degrees Celsius)

Orange Star:
9,000 degrees Fahrenheit
(4,900 degrees Celsius)

Red Star:
6,000 degrees Fahrenheit
(3,315 degrees Celsius)

80,000°F
70,000°F
60,000°F
50,000°F
40,000°F
30,000°F
20,000°F
10,000°F
0°F

Stars Die

Stars die when they run out of gas. It is like they are out of energy. They can't live anymore. When medium or small stars die, it is peaceful. Their outer layers blow off. The layers keep spreading. Eventually, there is nothing left.

The opposite is true for big stars. If you were up in space when a big star died, it would be like watching a fireworks show. The gas from the explosion would scatter across space.

Black Holes

When big stars explode, they can leave behind black holes. Black holes are like giant monsters in space. Their strong gravity pulls in anything that gets too close. They can swallow other stars and even planets. Stars and planets inside a black hole are broken apart and squashed into a tiny point.

17

Constellations

Stars stick together with other stars in space. A group of stars is called a constellation. There are 88 constellations in the sky. By connecting the stars that are near each other, we see patterns and shapes.

Stars move through space. This means constellations change over thousands of years. We can track them while studying the sky.

One of the most
famous constellations
is called The Big Dipper.

Can you see why it
has this name?

Look Up!

Gaze up into the night sky. Our universe is an amazing place. You'll spot many stars. Can you spot some of the patterns the stars make? Keep studying and exploring space. What you learn will be out of this world!

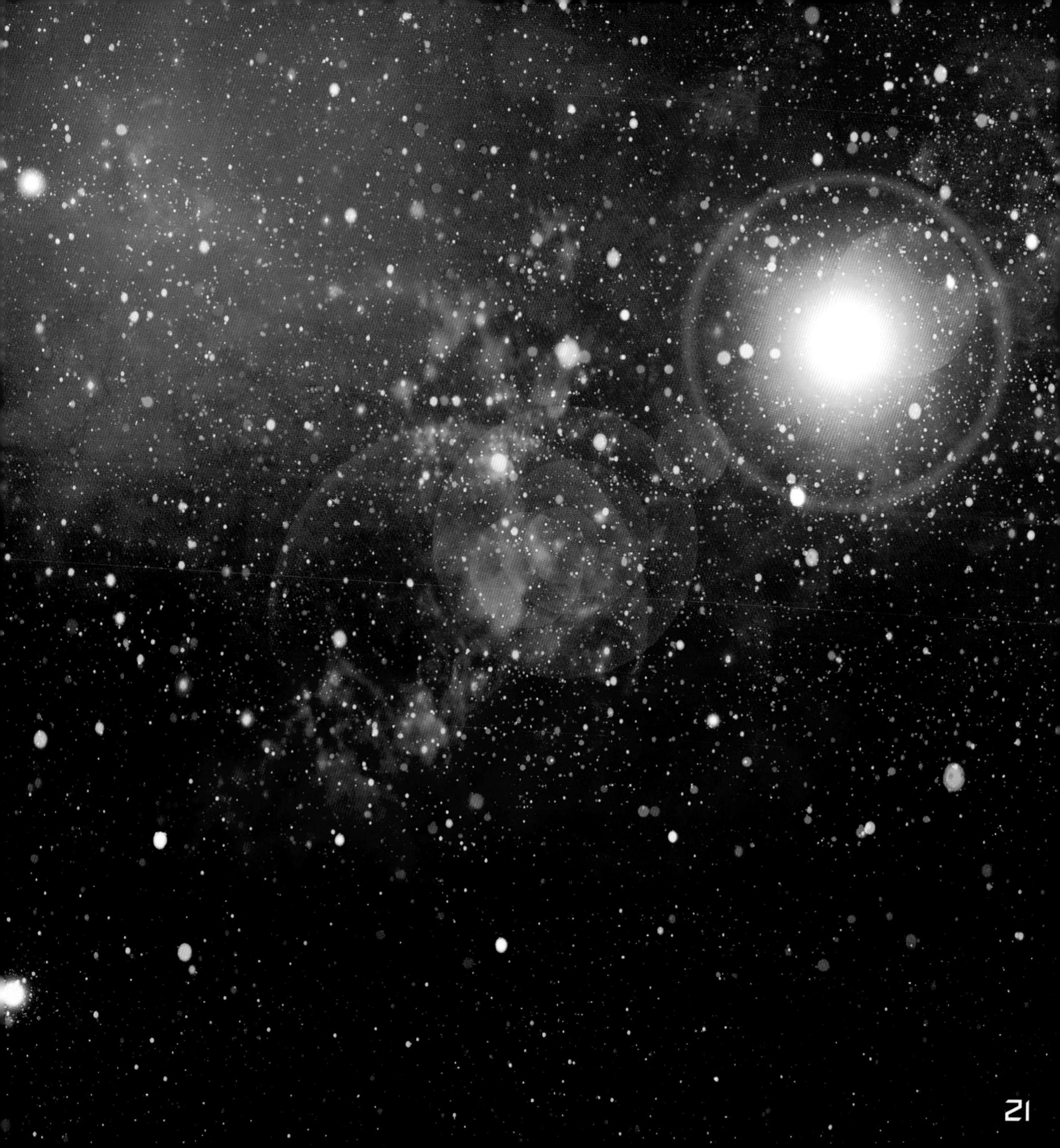

Glossary

energy (E-nuhr-jee)—the ability to do work, such as moving things or giving heat or light

gravity (GRAV-uh-tee)—a force that pulls objects together

hydrogen (HYE-druh-juhn)—a colorless, odorless, flammable gas

nebula (NEB-yuh-luh)—a cloud of dust and gas

orbit (OR-bit)—to travel around an object in space

scientist (SYE-un-tist)—an expert in the field of science

solar system (SOH-ler SIS-tuhm)—the sun and the eight planets and other bodies that revolve around it

telescope (TEL-uh-skhop)—a tool that makes faraway things look closer than they are

universe (YOO-nuh-vurs)—everything that exists, including the Earth, the stars, and all of space

Read More

Betts, Bruce. *Astronomy For Kids: How to Explore Outer Space with Binoculars, a Telescope, or Just Your Eyes!* Emeryville, California: Rockridge Press, 2018.

Green, Jen. *The Sun and Our Solar System.* Great Scientific Theories. North Mankato, MN: Capstone Press, 2018.

Seluk, Nick. *The Sun Is Kind of a Big Deal.* London: Orchard Books, 2018.

Internet Sites

NASA Kids' Club
https://www.nasa.gov/kidsclub/index.html

Space.com
https://www.space.com/

Critical Thinking Questions

- How big is our sun compared to other stars?

- What happens when a star dies?

- What is a constellation? How many are there in the sky?

Index